THE TWIN CITIES, NATURALLY
A Pictorial Tour of the Minneapolis–St. Paul Metropolitan Area

GREG RYAN & SALLY BEYER
INTRODUCTION BY MARCIA APPEL

VOYAGEUR PRESS

A note from the editor

In *The Twin Cities, Naturally*, you'll find short commentaries written by Twin Citians (and some former residents). We surveyed several hundred people, asking them what they like about the Twin Cities, and included the remarks that we received. Opening the mail on those days was a delight. We heard from many who consider the Twin Cities' natural spaces, cultural attractions, and vitality and ingenuousness of the people to be the best parts of the Cities. I couldn't agree more. I hope that you readers will remember some of your own favorite scenes or stories while browsing through these pages. If you're visiting, I hope you'll stop by many of these sites; you'll know why we like it here. Thank you to all who sent comments back, to Greg and Sally who picture these cities so beautifully, and to Marcia who wrote an introduction into which many of us Twin Citians can place ourselves.

≈≈≈

Introduction copyright © 1994 by Marcia Appel
Photographs and captions copyright © 1994 by Greg Ryan and Sally Beyer

Edited by Helene Anderson   ∽   Designed by Lou Gordon
Printed in Hong Kong
97 98   5   4   3   2

Library of Congress Cataloging-in-Publication Data
Ryan, Greg, 1944–
    The twin cities, naturally : a pictorial tour of the Minneapolis–St. Paul metropolitan
area / by Greg Ryan and Sally Beyer.
        p. cm.
    ISBN 0-89658-232-9
    1. Minneapolis (Minn.)—Pictorial works. 2. Saint Paul (Minn.)—Pictorial works.
    I. Beyer, Sally, 1948–   . II. Title.
    F614.M6R93   1994
    977.6'579—dc20   93-34642
                                                                          CIP

Published by VOYAGEUR PRESS, INC.
P.O. Box 338, 123 North Second Street, Stillwater, MN 55082 U.S.A. 612-430-2210

Please write or call, or stop by, for our free catalog of natural history publications. Our TOLL-FREE number to place an order or to obtain a free catalog is 800-888-9653.

Educators, fundraisers, premium and gift buyers, publicists, and marketing managers: Looking for creative products and new sales ideas? Voyageur Press books are available at special discounts when purchased in quantities, and special editions can be created to your specifications. For details contact our marketing department.

Page 1: With incredible foresight, civic leaders of early Minneapolis purchased the land surrounding the city's lakes for parks, walkways, and public roads, guaranteeing equal access for all. One of Minneapolis's earliest parks was on the shores of Lake Harriet, and its first pavilion and dance hall were built in 1888. Lake Harriet's newest pavilion or bandshell, and accompanying refectory, are pictured here. It looks peaceful in this early morning shot, but many hundreds of music lovers often show up for concerts held throughout the summer.

Opposite page, top: The State Capitol seen through a window in the Minnesota History Center. **Left:** Tie-dyed clothes for sale along St. Paul's Snelling Avenue. **Center:** Mural by Sara Rothholz Weiner on the Hiawatha Avenue grain elevator in South Minneapolis. **Right:** Freeways leading to the urban center of Minneapolis.

CONTENTS

Dedication

To our parents, John & Marie Ryan, and Liberty & Norman Beyer,
who always believed in us and gave us the strength to follow our dreams

In Minneapolis, Father Louis Hennepin Suspension Bridge spans the Mississippi River, the nation's first interior artery of commerce. Built on the site of the first permanent bridge across the entire river, the bridge was named after a Franciscan friar who came here in the late 1600s to chart maps for the curious kings and queens across the sea.

INTRODUCTION

*U*sually when I leave for work in the morning, I pull the car out of the driveway and head for the shortest, fastest route to the freeway. On most days I'm already trying to beat time by then, having passed a few hours feeding kids, sorting laundry, and answering mail. So if I dawdle and go "the long way"—past the ripe bogs, greening golf course, stands of fluttering prairie grass, marsh marigolds, and protected trees and wildlife areas—several extra minutes expand a commute that too often is harried and harrowing.

On certain mornings, however, the grand scenery of my Twin Cities town south of the Minnesota River calls me away from the sensible, speedy route. From time to time, I like to check out the progress of the new "executive" townhouses rising awkwardly from the hillsides facing the pristine lake in Murphy-Hanrehan Regional Park, a jewel of a biological sanctuary about thirty minutes from the urban wildlife of downtowns Minneapolis and St. Paul.

On one particular early summer morning—notable for its steady, dripping drizzle and unseasonably low temperatures—I cruised by the bruised housing site, muttering about the literal erosion of progress and the folly of developers' discovery. I rounded a sharp curve, and, as I eased out of its arc, a huge, lumbering snapping turtle slid out of the grass and down the curb, just to the right of my rapidly rolling front tire.

I slammed on the brakes and pulled to the side. I could see the hard-shelled creature in my rearview mirror, observing with alarm that he was determined to cross the street. In an instant, it came to me that this was not a "he" but a "she," one driven by a mothering instinct to move away from her lake home to claim a nesting place for her eggs. I jumped out of the idling car and ran as best as I could, given the weather conditions, to face the traveling tortoise. Predictably, it retreated into its shell, its tail tucked against my toe.

Bending over, rain dripping down my eyeglasses and then the tip of my nose, I grabbed onto the thick shell and heaved with all my might. But the turtle's size—and smarts—threw me off balance. As I worked to lift it even one inch from the slick concrete, its claws emerged to tear away my fingers, and a distinct hissing sound ascended. This turtle knew where it wanted to go and wasn't about to be thwarted by me. After a few seconds, I released the snapper and fled to my car to plan my next move. In this still-new,

career-woman's vehicle, I carried no tools, no gloves, no boots, nothing to help a stubborn turtle out of danger.

As I sat there stewing—who was this turtle to turn me away when I was trying to save its life?—the roar of a loud engine drew my eyes once again to my rearview mirror. Careering around the corner was a large cement truck, the back bowl mixing the cargo while the driver headed for his destiny—the invading townhouse development only a block away.

"Oh no," I thought to myself, "I've seen this kind before, these fast-driving, nature-offending construction workers." I held my breath, certain that the cement truck's rough-and-ready driver would purposely roll over the turtle just for some early-morning sport. I assumed that the only thing the working man and I had in common was that our vehicles, one utilitarian and one a low-slung roadster, both are painted white.

But wait! The speeding truck slid just in front of my sedan, and the driver—tanned, toned, turned out in bleached jeans and a blue-cotton shirt—jumped out and ran past me to take a look at the turtle, which still was inside its house, hissing and clawing as though the Third Army were advancing. In a repeat of my earlier failed performance, the driver knelt and also attempted to pick up the tortured turtle. In a few seconds he also retreated. As he jogged past my car, he paused momentarily to yell into the half-open window: "I've got a pail in my truck. Help me prod him into it. We've got to get him back to the lake before some goon runs him over." I was too stunned by my stereotyping assumption that played against this man's compassion and patience to mention that the "him" was actually a "her."

*T*he story of the turtle, once lost then saved, disappears in a tapestry woven of over 2,900 square miles in seven counties and 2.5 million human inhabitants, untold numbers of flora from wild orchids to towering pines, and fauna that delight the most seasoned naturalists and the most stoical urbanites. Yet for me it is a sweet reminder of the fragility and beauty of this area known simply around the country and some other parts of the world as the Twin Cities.

I love the Twin Cities. My first husband brought me here as a nineteen-year-old bride, and, while that teenage marriage didn't last, my passion for the Twin Cities took hold. I remember my inaugural trip to Minneapolis on the same night that a man took "One small step for man, one giant leap for mankind." While Neil Armstrong walked out onto the lunar surface, I circled over the Cities in a rumbling DC9, as much in awe of the miles of sparkling lights, ribbons of roads, and tree-edged disks of water as the astronaut might have been of the Man in the Moon. Later that same night, traveling on Minneapolis's freeways at speeds I considered stunning at best and unsafe at worst, I crinked my neck to peer at the Foshay Tower, never dreaming that twenty-some years later it would stand like a dwarf among skyscrapers once reserved, if only in my imagination, for the Big Apple or the Windy City. I vowed that night to travel each of its streets, to visit its many neighborhoods, to camp in its nearby wildernesses, to stand atop its tallest buildings, and to defend its most ancient sites. I adopted the Twin Cities as my hometown, and, like parents and children thrown together by choice or nature, the new relationship required some work, some wonder, and some forgiveness.

Over time, I have realized that the effort to protect that one turtle has been duplicated millions and millions of times over the last century and a half. These gestures have created an environment celebrated for both its strength and its extremes. From the northern edge of the metropolitan area, which now nudges the tree line that separates prairie from pines, to the black loam farm fields of the southern tip, the growing season varies by nearly a week. From the western boundaries along hobby farms and two-stories on two acres to the eastern side bordered by the pure, federally protected St. Croix River, lie in tandem the two famous downtowns of Minneapolis and St. Paul, their neighborhoods and reasons for being as different as I am from you.

𝓗ome for me in the Twin Cities always meant being on the move—an apartment in St. Paul, a townhouse in Cottage Grove, a "grown-up house" in Eden Prairie, a summer cottage on the Upper St. Croix River, a swank career-woman's co-op up the street from the Guthrie Theater, right beneath the lighted green-blue steeple of Hennepin Avenue United Methodist Church and, perhaps, under the nose of God himself. And now I live in Lakeville, surrounded by a blockful of kids, a pond in the backyard, stands of oaks, and the lowing—the *lowing,* mind you—of cows. In every place, I have witnessed the drama of ordinary life played out in extraordinary scope. As my own life unfolded, so did the life—and the size—of the Twin Cities. Now, like the turtle who takes her house with her whenever she moves, I find my home wherever I land in this particular geosphere.

But no matter where the letter carrier has dropped my mail in these Twin Cities, the siren's songs of the fast and slow lanes called to me with equal intensity. Because I was raised on a small Iowa working farm, solitude and square miles of crop and pasturelands comfort me and give me rest when I so badly need it. A well for pure water, one high-voltage yard light, tractors instead of horses, a neighbor or two on the same section of land, *Life* magazine and the daily newspaper—these were the luxuries of my young life on the vast prairie.

But the Twin Cities opened up other possibilities. Energy. Music. Feminism. Theater. Sports. Dance. Jobs. Knowledge. Debate. Relationships. The coming together of hundreds and hundreds of thousands of persons to create and recreate the institutions, traditions, and events that over time come to mean community. All these were the greeting cards handed to me.

Like so many others who moved here, I took advantage of the great educational prowess of the region. My first day at the University of Minnesota stood in stark contrast to every other day of my life up until then. Surrounded by 45,000 other students on this river-banked campus—easily fifteen times as many as I lived with in my hometown—I surveyed, shyly at first and then with great vigor, the offerings of an institution that some historians describe as the engine of Minnesota.

The great university showed me a world beyond the rim of the known and, within its borders, introduced me to radical ideas at both extremes—and some right down the middle. It forced together different kinds of people who might otherwise have ignored each other. It demanded that you know something of the here and now as well as of the past, and it is not a cliché to say that it teemed with thought and action. I studied in its cloistered libraries, sipped brew at the adjacent student coffeehouses, observed the gigantic upheavals of my time—Vietnam, Watergate, the rights movement—and then slipped back into the larger community to make sense of it all. I found that the Twin Cities' student body—not just of the University but also of the University of St. Thomas, the College of St. Catherine, Macalester College, Hamline University, Metro State University, William Mitchell Law College, and dozens of other schools in this area—forms a collective that pushes the envelope of politics, entrepreneurship, religion, of culture itself.

In those four student years and now as an adjunct professor at the beloved school that is too often misunderstood and sometimes misguided, I put aside time to delve into the mysteries and complexities ignored in everyday life. This school and all the others, with their museums, and musi-

A patch of marsh marigolds, also called cowslips, are a bright addition to the spring landscape in St. Paul's Battle Creek Park . The park includes the site of many battles between Dakota and Ojibway in 1842.

cians, their institutes, their lectures, and their insistent urges to stir the pot, enrich my life. Each time I drive onto one of the campuses, I feel a little safer, content to know that were there are books and classrooms, and the intermingling of generations, genders, races, and attitudes, there also is hope.

Since those student days, I have wandered like a nomad along the byways of the Twin Cities. When I was younger, I worried that one year there would be nothing left to see or do here, no new territory to explore, no new cause to champion, no new position to achieve. Way back then, I assumed that at some point I would migrate to a place with brighter lights, fatter paychecks, taller buildings, greater numbers of art houses, factories, restaurants, magazines, newspapers, opportunities.

Twenty-five years later, I'm still here. Each day I meet someone else who came as a youngster and created a jigsaw puzzle too complicated to leave easily. With great regularity I talk to people who grew up in the Twin Cities and eagerly left, only to find themselves coping with a deep homesickness some years later.

My own dear friend abandoned Minneapolis in her early thirties, drawn by her new husband to the strangeness and raciness of Manhattan. Those were heady years. On regular visits there, we attended the openings of Broadway plays, shopped from Uptown haute couture to Village grunge, feasted on the temples of good food blessed by one critic or another. But I always was so glad to come home. As I traveled farther in the world, I saw that the Twin Cities incubated businesses, ideas, products, music, plays, books, and yes, talent that could be exported. Broadway may be bright, but how many people know that several of its major theaters are owned and nurtured by a Twin Citian? Our own theaters—Mixed Blood, Penumbra, Illusion, Children's, Guthrie, Teatro del Pueblo, and dozens of others—draw thousands of tourists and give work to exquisitely skilled writers, actors, and directors.

A stroll through the Walker Art Museum and its sculpture garden, a concert at Orchestra Hall, a dash into Olde England at the Renaissance Festival, a class at the Minnesota Landscape Arboretum, a day at the Minnesota History Center, a Twins or Vikings or Timberwolves game, a meeting in the Warehouse District, a ride on a Mississippi paddlewheeler—they all remind me that the Twin Cities are still young, still in the messy process of defining themselves. That is their main attraction. When you move to or visit the Twin Cities, you can make a difference, get in on something new, contribute to change because there's still room, still a chance to shine.

Driven by immigration of people from other states and other countries, the Twin Cities each year lose some of their Wonderbread status. The arrival of Hmong, African-Americans, Hispanics, and so many others alters the original Native American–Scandinavian–German blend and gives rise to new art forms, new cuisines, new music, new celebrations, new economic vigor. As the texture changes, so do the descriptions. No longer white bread and fry bread, we are content to become pumpernickel. Pumpernickel with conversation about the weather as gluten.

You can't talk about the Twin Cities for very long without mentioning the weather. Extremely hot and humid. Extremely frigid and snowy. Extremely stormy. Extremely sunny—unless, of course, it's extremely cloudy. The weather, though, provides an apt metaphor for the extremes that run throughout life in Minnesota in general and the Twin Cities in particular. Consider these strange Twin Cities bedfellows: The Center for the American Experiment, a conservative thinktank, and the Hubert H. Humphrey Institute, a monument to liberal thought. Prince and Garrison Keillor. An industry built around helping people recover from addictions and a booming industry that hypes gambling on every corner. Peregrine falcons nesting atop downtown Minneapolis sky-high buildings. Parks and wetlands nestled up against four-lane superhighways. I've come to believe that the extremes of winter and summer here—and don't forget the mosquitoes—forced people to be nicer to each other and, in the end, also more tolerant of each other. Polarized by snowstorms and tornadoes, Twin Citians developed attitudes, talents, and organizations that also covered the gamut.

When people visit me, they marvel at the friendliness of clerks and waitstaff, stare with disbelief at the fine public spaces spawned by one generation and preserved and expanded by another, roll their eyes at the heated political debates that oftentimes have helped set the national agenda, stood in line to get into one of the country's oldest and largest state fairs, ogled the wares at the farmer's markets, been impressed by the number of bikers, runners, Rollerbladers, ice skaters, skiers, and dog-walkers. Nothing stops Twin Citians, not the snow, not the heat, not the problems, and certainly not the solutions. Early on the pioneers of this area learned that they couldn't beat the weather so they joined it. These days, modern Twin Citians act in much the same way whether it means strapping on cross-country skies or passing legislation. Outsiders have called this approach Pollyanna.

We call it extremely efficient.

Life goes full circle and so it has for me. Only a few months ago, sitting in the fast lane of Interstate 35W, southbound for home and the weekend, the traffic slowed to an agonizing creep. Already seven o'clock in the evening, it was hard to believe that many people were heading for the Mall of America or Lakeville.

A few yards past an intersecting freeway, a woman in a white car pulled over to the left side—the wrong side—of the freeway and jumped out of her car. There, running dead center down the busiest roadway in the state, were six ducklings, not more than a few days old. Each car crept by the terrified babies, driving with desperate care to avoid crushing their fuzzy, quivering bodies. The woman, standing for the briefest time in the median, raised her right arm with the best authority of an experienced traffic cop and stopped the first lane of traffic. Then the second. Then the third and finally the fourth. A few drivers honked, but most waited courteously as she herded the flock to the other side and the safety of the tall grass. Once there, she grabbed for the ducklings but came up short-handed with only four. Clutching them to her pink linen blouse, she searched fruitlessly for the other two, tracking their peeps like sonar. Forty-five minutes later, still with only four ducks, which now had stained her top into a greenish cast, she gave up.

Just then two cars pulled over. The first, a Jeep with Minnesota plates, carried a young couple. "Need help?" one of them asked. "I can't find these other two ducklings," the woman said. "Don't worry," the other Jeep passenger replied. "We'll stay until we capture them." As the woman passed a second stopped vehicle—this one a van from Missouri—the driver leaned out and said, "Do you need help?"

"You don't have a box, do you?" the woman asked. Through the window, like a gift, came a box just deep and wide enough to hold four frightened ducklings. The woman placed her catch into the box and gave the little kids in the van just one peek. Then, with her left arm extended, she again stopped four lanes of zooming interstate traffic with the understanding of most everyone involved and climbed back into her white roadster.

Only hours later did the woman understand the deeper meaning of the whole event. For one brief time in her long and winding journey, the fast and slow lanes of life in the Twin Cities had merged. In a moment of compassion and patience, thousands of people surrendered to inconvenience to protect some mystical balance that exists between nature and city in a place called home.

Marcia Appel

On the 700 block of Minneapolis's Hennepin Avenue, this neon-wrapped fire escape exemplifies the mixture of old and new, traditional and nontraditional, found in this area. The early-1900s building housed the extensive Witt's Market House until the sixties and was the home of Dinty Moore hams, produced in the market's own smokehouse. Now the building houses a Musicland store; the chain's headquarters are located in St. Louis Park, southwest of downtown.

THE HEARTS OF THE CITIES
The Downtowns and Beyond

"*The Minneapolis and St. Paul metropolitan area epitomizes for me the American urban ideal. Not even winter can dampen my zeal for living here. It's as if there were an unwritten pact among Twin Citians to insure the livability of this metropolis.*" **Carol M. Robertshaw, Writer/Artist/Director, ArtWord, and Producer/ Host, KUOM Radio**

Opposite top: After a devastating fire in 1982 destroyed their headquarters, Norwest Corporation made a bold statement of commitment to downtown Minneapolis by constructing this dramatic building, called the Norwest Center, on Marquette Avenue. Designed by Cesar Pelli, Norwest Center is distinguished by sweeping vertical lines and covered by native Kasota stone, which draw the eye ever upward. Against this prestorm sky, its reflective surface casts myriad colors and shapes. Be sure to check out Norwest Center at night, from a bit of a distance. Its exterior lighting has been lauded as a public work of art.

Opposite left: This area of downtown Minneapolis along the Mississippi River near Father Louis Hennepin Bridge is teeming with history, though it now seems just a pleasant place for a morning jog. When the power of the nearby St. Anthony Falls was first commercially contained by soldiers from Fort Snelling and then by settlers from the east, this area saw a small community of lumber mills, followed by a very large community of flour mills. The northern forests became depleted, competitive flour mills rose else-where, and this became a skid row of flophouses, bars, and Salvation Army food lines. Local leaders finally took action, and much of the river front has now been revitalized. Here you will find parks, walking and biking paths, an excursion boat, and first-class stores, restaurants, and hotels, many in renovated buildings.

Opposite center: Nicollet Mall is the main artery of Minneapolis's shopping district, and it provides a pedestrian-friendly way to see downtown Minneapolis. Covering twelve blocks, the mall offers a wide variety of small shops and restaurants, department stores such as Dayton's, Saks Fifth Avenue, Neiman Marcus, and Montgomery Ward, and entrance to four large shopping complexes. Closed to most vehicles, the mall is part of an extended walkway of nearly two miles, beginning just south of the Mississippi River and ending near the nationally acclaimed Guthrie Theater. City busses regularly run along the mall, so you can walk as much as you want and then ride back to where you started.

Opposite right: An oasis of colorful flowers greets visitors to the Minneapolis Convention Center, a recent addition to the downtown area that is drawing a steady stream of business. Plantings at the Convention Center include 6,000 annuals and thousands of perennials, and cover more than 45,000 square feet.

Above: Despite cold winters, Minneapolis has created a good climate in other ways for convention planners. Topping the list of options is the Minneapolis Convention Center, an attractive and well-planned building housing nearly 280,000 square feet of exhibit space, two ballrooms, and numerous meeting rooms. Located near the south end of Marquette Avenue, the Convention Center is close to major hotels, fine dining and shopping, small theaters and Orchestra Hall, and is only a few blocks from other downtown attractions.

The moon looks down on the Romanesque-style clock tower of the old Hennepin County Courthouse, now just a tiny part of sky-scraping downtown Minneapolis, which includes the IDS Center (the city's tallest building, at 775 feet), Norwest Center, International Centre, and Piper Jaffray Tower. The ghosts reputed to inhabit the old courthouse must wonder what has happened to the old town. In the center of the photo is the Foshay Tower, listed on the National Register of Historic Places. Completed in 1929, the thirty-two-story tower was the tallest building in Minneapolis until 1973. You can visit the observation deck and the Wilbur Foshay Tower Museum, where you can learn how to go from $200 to $60 million and back to zero, as Mr. Foshay did!

Above: One of the many bridges spanning the Mississippi River in the Twin Cities area is the Third Avenue–Central Avenue Bridge, which links two historic milling districts. Although we may cross the river routinely now, until 1855 the trip included a ferry ride through rushing waters, dodging floating logs along the way.

Top inset: One of the newest sports and entertainment locales is Target Center on the northwest side of downtown Minneapolis. Target Center is home to Minnesota's professional basketball team, the Timberwolves. Whenever the "Wolves" don't have a home game, this state-of-the-art arena is apt to be hosting a circus, ice show, professional tennis match, or concert by a nationally known artist. Travel below the arena and you will find a complete health and fitness club with running track, pool, and racquet/handball and (of course!) basketball courts.

14

Center inset: Fans head for the Hubert H. Humphrey Metrodome in downtown Minneapolis for the first Vikings football game of the season. The Minnesota Vikings may well have initiated the construction of the "Dome," hinting they might move on to a warmer climate if one was not built. Since its opening in the early 1980s, the Dome has proven a success, being the site of the Superbowl, two World Series, and the NCAA Final Four, bringing welcome dollars to downtown Minneapolis.

Bottom inset: A young fan shows whose side he's on outside the Metrodome, home to Minnesota's professional baseball team, the Minnesota Twins. The Twin Cities has had a big league baseball team since the early 1960s, and Twins games draw a large following of faithful fans. In 1987 and 1991, the Twins won the World Series Championship, and the roar of the crowd was deafening in downtown Minneapolis, coming right through the ten-acre, hot-air-inflated roof of the dome.

Right: Holiday decorations brighten downtown Minneapolis, like these in front of the Metropolitan Centre (called Lincoln Centre until January 1994). A thirty-one-story office building on Fourth Avenue South, the Metropolitan Centre adds a post-modern touch to the skyline.

Below: The bustling downtown area of Minneapolis is dominated by reaching-to-the-sky office buildings. Thankfully, midwestern common sense and respect for the past prevailed during Minneapolis's several building booms, and many examples of fine old architecture have been saved. The dramatic lines and colors of the Norwest Center and the AT&T Tower blend beautifully here with the reminder of an earlier era.

"From the banks of the St. Croix River to the heights of the stunning Norwest Center in downtown Minneapolis; from the farmland of the northern suburbs to St. Paul's Ordway Music Theater. What other metropolitan area offers such an amazing mixture of big-city life and rural pleasures? Yet it is the people who choose to live in the Twin Cities that serve as our greatest treasure." **Rod Grams, United States Congressman, Minnesota Sixth District**

Left: The interior of Gaviidae Common is festooned with artful Christmas decorations. This upscale complex covers two blocks along Minneapolis's Nicollet Mall and offers Neiman Marcus and Saks Fifth Avenue department stores and over sixty specialty stores and restaurants. Identifying with its Minnesota location, the name *Gaviidae Common* translates roughly from Latin into "common loon," the Minnesota state bird.

Below: Just a few blocks from the Mississippi River, this fountain presents a colorful water show in front of the Northwestern National Life Company. Officially called Gateway Park, this area was once the pride and joy of Minneapolis, a thriving center of commercial activity. Over the years it went downhill and by the 1930s it was referred to as "hobohemia." Nearly two hundred buildings were torn down in the 1960s, and the area was rebuilt with modern office buildings and high-rise condominiums, making it once again a vital part of downtown Minneapolis.

"No matter what the call for volunteer aid or community support, our citizens rise to the occasion and get the job done. And this includes all corners of our community—the elderly using their newly acquired free time, parents volunteering in their children's schools and park programs, new residents and lifelong neighbors coming forth to help their particular groups or the general community. I feel sure that this spirit and tradition will continue to flourish here." **Donald M. Fraser, Former Mayor, City of Minneapolis**

Left: The 1908 Ceresota Elevator, its interior redone as office space, shares historic real estate along the Mississippi River in Minneapolis with the four-star Whitney Hotel. This area, together with the bank across the river, supported a dozen mills by 1870, making Minneapolis the nation's leading producer of flour until the 1930s. In fact, Minneapolis was known as "Mill City." Flour milling triggered Minnesota's growth more than any single industry. Most of the families who profited from flour milling reinvested in the Twin Cities over the years to create a strong, culturally diverse community.

Opposite, bottom left: This mural of Venice, painted by Herman Krumpholz, can be found on the Gluek's Bar & Restaurant building in Minneapolis's warehouse district. The charm and vibrancy of this painting is representative of what you will find in this popular fourteen-block area at the northwestern corner of downtown. Wonderful old brick buildings have been remodeled into theaters, restaurants, night clubs, and art galleries, with loving attention to preserving fine details and lines. Most of the 157 buildings and brick and cobblestone streets are listed on the National Register of Historic Places, many dating from the late 1800s and early 1900s. Though you won't exactly slip back in time here, with throbbing Hennepin Avenue one block away, you will find an ambiance resulting from the mixture of the best of the past with the best of the present.

Opposite, bottom right: This winter view of the Minneapolis skyline is from the plaza of the Whitney Mill Quarter office complex, created from the 1879 Crown Roller Mill, one of more than a dozen flour mills that once operated in this area. A few steps away is the Mississippi River, a Lock & Dam Visitor Center, and the now much-diminished St. Anthony Falls. Once a powerful jumble of rushing water, a wide limestone ledge, boulders, and islands, the waterfall fueled the lumber and flour mills that cemented Minneapolis as a major commercial center.

Below left: This neon sign very simply, but colorfully, tells you what you will find in the "Mississippi Mile," just across the river from Minneapolis's main downtown area. With its roots in the power of the river and the flour and lumber mills that flourished here, the district today offers fifteen hot night spots at Mississippi Live, comedy clubs, galleries, shops, and great food at St. Anthony Main and Riverplace.

Below right: What better way to explore the Mississippi Mile than by horse and carriage? The beginnings of Minneapolis commerce took place right here on the east bank of the Mississippi. The town was once named St. Anthony due to its proximity to St. Anthony Falls (that neighborhood still uses the name). In the 1840s, this side of the river was the settlers' downtown district, an area of mills, offices, and warehouses, and the native Dakota lived across the river on the west bank. In 1851, St. Anthony listed over seven hundred residents, while the site that would become Minneapolis listed fifteen. In the 1970s, many of the original buildings in the old St. Anthony area were beautifully restored and now house restaurants, nightclubs, specialty stores, and offices. There are parks and pathways, benches and picnic tables, with numerous views of the river, cobblestone streets, old bridges, an amphitheater, and French meat pies for sale at Our Lady of Lourdes Church.

Right: A cold seat affords a sunset view of Minneapolis from Ridgeway Parkway. Minneapolis and St. Paul lie halfway between the equator and the North Pole, near the center of North America.

Below: A man finds respite from a hard day of work in the skyscrapers of downtown Minneapolis by traveling a few miles southwest to Lake Harriet, renting a canoe, and heading out to his favorite fishing spot with his dog. One of seventeen lakes in Minneapolis, Harriet is surrounded by beautiful homes and loved and attended by urban dwellers who appreciate the oasis it offers.

"I love Minneapolis and can't imagine living anyplace else. Where else could I walk around my neighborhood lake and then drive fifteen minutes to the theater? This juxtaposition of urban culture and the great outdoors is wonderful and uniquely Minneapolis." **Catherine Shreves, President, Minneapolis League of Women Voters**

"My favorite sight is driving into downtown St. Paul on I-94 westbound after being away for awhile. Coming around the corner and seeing the city lit up — the Cathedral on one side and the Capitol on the other — it feels as though it was all put on to welcome me home." **Kristin Cooper, Office Manager, College of St. Catherine**

Top: Sparkling new headquarters of the St. Paul Companies marks the terminus of Seventh Place Mall, a developing area of shops and cafes in downtown St. Paul, and a pleasant place to enjoy coffee and the paper. The St. Paul Companies, originally St. Paul Fire & Marine Insurance, has been in business since 1853, five years before Minnesota became a state. The company began its business as an insurer of goods traveling by steamboat on the Mississippi River.

Bottom: People in the Twin Cities got smart several years ago and built enclosed skyways or skywalks between major office and retail buildings. Though skyways have their critics, these heated and air-conditioned passageways have made life much easier for downtown workers, visitors, and residents. Our ancestors probably would have approved wholeheartedly. This image of a St. Paul skyway includes a golden view of the St. Paul Cathedral, just west of downtown.

Opposite: Freeway overpass view of the skyline of St. Paul at dusk. The World Trade Center is St. Paul's tallest building at present. The downtown St. Paul business area is separated from the State Capitol area by the freeway system. Many attractive and user-friendly bridges, which were recently rebuilt to reflect the traditional architecture common to St. Paul, make the division less formidable.

"Nowhere else is the living so easy and yet so full. This is a rare metropolitan area because it has all of the advantages of a huge city — entertainment, sports, shopping, the great outdoors — and few of the disadvantages." **Mindi Keirnan, Managing Editor–News, St. Paul Pioneer Press**

Top: At the western edge of the downtown business district, St. Paul's Civic Center plays host to a variety of conventions, concerts, and special events. The Civic Center offers 180,000 square feet, including an auditorium, arena, and trade show areas.

Bottom: The passage of time is reflected in this image. Since 1855, a brewery has been located on this site, and the tower of the Schmidt Brewery became a familiar sight in St. Paul around 1900. Schmidt supported many working-class families in the modest, tightly knit communities surrounding it. But competition took its toll in the late 1980s, and the brewery was sold and changed names in 1991. The new Minnesota Brewing Company chose "Landmark" as the name of its signature beer, and a new sign appeared against the sky.

Opposite: Shooting up about fifty-seven feet approximately every two minutes, this indoor fountain is a neck-stretcher. As you look up, you will see the soaring form of the thirty-six-story World Trade Center, St. Paul's tallest building and the city's hope for strong international commerce. You can find the fountain in a retail area adjacent to the World Trade Center lobby.

"Because the Twin Cities are friendly and accessible, they are the biggest small towns in America — or, depending upon your perspective, the smallest big cities in America. They aren't without the problems of big cities, but somehow the problems seem manageable. People in the fast-track here still operate within the speed limit. They care about their community, and are proud of it." **Brian Anderson, Editor,** Mpls.St.Paul *magazine*

Far left, top: Flowers in one of St. Paul's first parks, Smith (now called Mears Park), one square block in the downtown area. Early settlers were determined to preserve this block of land, setting it aside in 1849. Mears Park contains over eight thousand wildflowers, perennials, and ornamental grasses, as well as patches of birch and pine and a bench waiting just for you.

Far left, bottom: A dramatic blend of history, religion, and modern business is reflected in this small corner of the St. Paul skyline. The rooflines and steeples of the 1909 St. Louis Catholic and 1889 Central Presbyterian churches are shown against the backdrop of Galtier Plaza, a mix of retail, office, and residential spaces. This co-existence of contrasts is representative of St. Paul's mixture of people, religions, and interests.

Left: From the end of April to the middle of November, St. Paulites can get fresh Minnesota products like these cucumbers every weekend at the Farmers' Market. Located in the Lower-town area of downtown St. Paul, the Farmers' Market guarantees that everything sold is produced within a fifty-mile radius. In addition to in-season produce, you can find honey, herbs, poultry, plants, bagel sandwiches, and more. Not shown here, the Minneapolis Farmer's Market also attracts crowds of those who prefer locally grown produce, fresh flowers, and handiwork.

Below: Combining healthy food with good exercise, a St. Paul woman returns from an excursion to a local farmers' market with bike baskets full of apples, squash, and corn. Scenes like this tell you why the Twin Cities continually ranks so high in national surveys for overall quality of life.

Top: A bright and inviting spot on a cold November night, Mickey's Diner is the diner of yesterday tenaciously clinging to its tiny spot of real estate in downtown St. Paul. Built in 1938, Mickey's is now listed on the National Register of Historic Places. Open twenty-four hours a day, and definitely not offering cholesterol-free dining, Mickey's is an interesting place to observe St. Paul and its people.

Bottom: From John Ireland Boulevard, named in honor of the great leader of the Catholic population of Minnesota, St. Paul's skyline includes the sparkling new St. Paul Companies building, the twin peaks of the historic Assumption Catholic Church, the clock tower of the Landmark Center, and the glass-sheathed Landmark Towers. St. Paul is smaller in population than Minneapolis, with an almost European ambience. Walking its downtown streets, you don't feel rushed or hurried along by crowds. The skyscrapers are modest and few in number, and often you can see the sky and feel the sun on your shoulders.

Surely one of the most interesting and attractive areas of downtown St. Paul, Rice Park is bounded by the Ordway Music Theatre, the historic Landmark Center, the St. Paul Hotel, and the Public and James J. Hill Reference Libraries (not shown). Deeded to the city in 1849 by Henry Rice, the park originally had to contend with wandering cows and rug-beating housewives from the neighborhood. Today Rice Park offers music, art, history, literature, and fine food and lodging in one neat bundle, and St. Paul is justly proud of its "cultural square."

Top: Fine art can be found throughout the Twin Cities area, including on the grounds of General Mills's suburban headquarters. Shown here is *Torus Orbicularis major* by John Newman, created from cast and fabricated aluminum. General Mills was founded in 1928 and is famous for such familiar names as Cheerios, Wheaties, and Betty Crocker. Locally, General Mills is recognized as a civic-minded "mover and shaker."

Bottom: The impressive Carlson Towers in suburban Minnetonka exemplify the strong work ethic and determination of Minnesotans. The Carlson Companies today is a $5-billion-plus international company involved in a wide variety of services, the astounding success story of a twenty-three-year-old soap salesman named Curtis Carlson. He developed and grew the Gold Bond Stamp Company with a lot of ingenuity and hard work, and he never looked back.

"I admire the extraordinary can-do attitude of Twin Cities entrepreneurs. It's little wonder that our area has such a diverse, vibrant economy." **Terry G. Fiedler, Editor, Corporate Report Minnesota** *magazine*

Left: Swirling colors of the Americana Carousel in Knott's Camp Snoopy, the largest indoor amusement park in the United States, and smack dab in the middle of the awesome Mall of America. A spot for year-round fun, Camp Snoopy has sixteen rides, and some of them will make big kids scream along with the little ones, like the roller coaster flying sixty feet above the camp, covering 2,700 feet in two and one-half minutes, or the log chute with watery drops of forty feet. Lots of tamer rides are available too. Paul Bunyan and his Blue Ox, Babe, are in residence to greet the kids. Our lumberjack ancestors created the character of Paul Bunyan for their amusement, and children of the North Country have been hearing of his feats ever since.

Below: Entrance to a power shopping experience, the incredible Mall of America. Located south of Minneapolis in Bloomington, the mall is 2,468,000 square feet of retail space and more than 240 stores at last count, the largest complex of its kind in the United States.

"Twin Cities volunteers are dynamic, innovative, and generous. After nearly fifteen years at the United Way of Minneapolis Area, I believe Twin Citians are the best volunteers in the country. Their spirit, generosity, and drive continually challenge our organization to be more effective and achieve better results each year. This is a great place to live, and, for me personally, an even better place to work." **James C. Colville, President, United Way of Minneapolis Area**

Top: Life Link III provides twenty-four-hour critical care transport to and from any medical facility in the region. Two airplanes are also available for transport to anywhere in the nation. A nurse/paramedic team accompanies each and every flight. Here a patient is being delivered to the Children's Hospital of St. Paul for specialized treatment.

Center: Gleaming headquarters of Medtronic, Inc., in suburban Minneapolis. The company's founder, Earl Bakken, developed the world's first wearable, battery-powered cardiac pacemaker, and Medtronic is now one of the world's largest manufacturers of implant-able pacing devices. Companies like Medtronic have helped spawn a major medical-device industry here, resulting in the Twin Cities area often being referred to as "medical alley."

Opposite bottom: This Dayton's store in Edina's Southdale Shopping Center, modern as it looks, has its roots deeply embedded in Minnesota retailing history. At the turn of the century, George Draper Dayton opened his first store on Nicollet Avenue, where it still operates today. Nearly fifty years later, his grandsons, responding to the major movement of population to the suburbs, would develop Southdale, the nation's first all-enclosed, all-weather shopping mall, with Dayton's as the key retailer. The rest is history, and Dayton's continues to be the predominant retailer in the area.

Above: In the summer, fields of brown-eyed susans add sunny color to the Hyland Lake Park Reserve. Located in the city of Bloomington and just a quick drive from the heart of Minneapolis or the Mall of America, Hyland annually attracts some 450,000 visitors to its family-oriented nature programs and extensive recreation facilities.

Left: The Twin Cities is home to Northwest Airlines. Flights continuously depart from Minneapolis/St. Paul International Airport, south of downtown Minneapolis. The airport serves several other airlines and freight carriers, but Northwest offers the greatest number of domestic and international flights, as well as air link service to several smaller cities and towns.

Below: Headquarters of 3M Company (Minnesota Mining & Manufacturing) in suburban St. Paul. Beginning as a very small business in 1902 on the shores of Lake Superior, 3M hoped to make it big with a sandpaper-like product. It did, and 3M is now the largest employer in Minnesota, based on payroll, with over 23,000 employees in Minnesota alone. An international company now involved in manufacturing a diverse line of products, 3M ranks eleventh in earnings of the Fortune 500 companies and is ranked the fourth "most admired" company.

Right: The Mississippi River is a shining border along the edge of Minneapolis's business district, a vibrant reminder of the city's past. At Boom Island Park, this small lighthouse greets river visitors to the boat launch and Anson Northrup excursion boat landing. The twenty-five-acre park also has picnic shelters, a playground, and walking and hiking paths.

SPRING GREEN & WINTER WHITE
The Natural Areas in the Cities

"*To me, the Twin Cities' lakes and parks are a constant source of beauty and bliss. They inspire, comfort, and awaken our souls to the cycles of creation. I think we all become a little more alive when we're outside—especially when a fishing rod bends in our hands or the music of the marsh fills our ears.*" **Rod Sando, Commissioner,**

Minnesota Department of Natural Resources

Opposite top: Minneapolis owes its name to water—*minne* is Dakota for "water," and *polis* is Greek for "city." We might say the added *a* is for "attitude," one that said a beautiful city could be built that paid great respect to its lakes and parks. When you ask Minneapolitans (or would be's) their reasons for liking it here, they will nearly always include "the beautiful lakes and parks" in their answers. This young man fishing for muskie, walleye, or sunfish on Lake Harriet wouldn't want to live anywhere else.

Opposite left: Summer flowers and the small interactions of nature can be found in the heart of Minneapolis at Lyndale Farmstead Park and Thomas Sadler Roberts Bird Sanctuary, just north of Lake Harriet. Minneapolis has about 170 parks, which means you're never too far from a little green space.

Opposite center: A fun way to visit two Minneapolis innercity lakes is by way of the Harriet-Como Streetcar Line; the two-mile round trip takes fifteen minutes. You might marvel that city planners at one time thought of linking lakes Harriet and Calhoun. You can catch a ride every day all summer long, or on weekends until November.

Opposite right: This unusual fountain can be found in Lyndale Rose and Rock Garden, also called simply Lyndale Park, adjacent to Lake Harriet in Minneapolis. It was purchased by prominent Minneapolis businessman Frank Heffelfinger in 1925 from a villa near Florence, Italy. The sculptor is unknown, but stories from that time say he obviously was influenced by Florentine masters such as da Vinci, Michelangelo, de Vries, Bernini, and Donatello.

Above: The famous Minnehaha Falls, "laughing waters," immortalized in Henry Wadworth Longfellow's "The Song of Hiawatha," published in 1855. Although Longfellow's poem undoubtedly was a great advertisement for Minnesota, the falls were a tourist attraction three decades before the poem was published. Artists, authors, tour groups, honeymooners, teachers, and travelers of all sorts came by steamboat up the Mississippi to see, paint, or write about the falls. "How beautiful the name, for it is a wild, wild laugh you hear. . . . Nature speaks, and you are silent," wrote Harriet Bishop in a book published in 1857. Today Minnehaha Falls is surrounded by a park of towering trees, hiking and biking paths, and picnic tables.

Top: Sports are big in Minnesota, and running is right up there in popularity. With two major marathons each year in Minnesota, the Twin Cities Marathon and Grandma's in Duluth, you'll see lots of people training for a big race. Or maybe they just ate too many Swedish meatballs or German bratwurst for dinner. This group is circling Minneapolis's Lake Harriet. They're filling their lungs with fresh air, viewing a beautiful summer sunset, and visiting with friends and neighbors.

Center: Despite the fact Minnesota has a short growing season — or maybe because of it — people here love flowers, and you will see gardens, big and small, formal and informal, everywhere. The Lyndale Park Rose & Rock Gardens in south Minneapolis offer the kind of roses we all wish we could grow.

Below: To grow up in Minneapolis often means learning how to ice skate. When you can't swim in the water, you skate upon it. This young lad tests the strength of his ankles on a small rink at Riverplace, a retail and entertainment complex on the Mississippi River in a neighborhood full of history. Within walking distance of the main business district, across the river, this area is drawing many downtown workers to its high-rise condominiums for low-mileage living.

Right: A serene view of the Mississippi River at dawn belies the fact that just a short trip up the shoreline, cars rush over bridges, carrying workers to their jobs in nearby downtown Minneapolis. Planes fly overhead, and the Cities hum and roar and move. And the river rolls peacefully along.

Top: The beauty of a Japanese garden can be found behind Normandale Community College in Bloomington, the third-largest city in Minnesota. The two-acre hill garden was designed by Takao Watanabe. The small red bentendo and curved bridge were funded by the Nisei Military Intelligence Language School Veterans. They formed a corps of Japanese-Americans, trained in the Minneapolis area, who offered translation services to U.S. armed forces during World War II.

Bottom: In winter many Twin Citians head for local cross-country ski trails, like this fellow enjoying a run through Hyland Lake Park Reserve in Bloomington. Hennepin County has thirteen parks in the park reserve system, with more than 140 kilometers of cross-country ski trails. All that exercise and fresh air must do some good—Minnesotans are second only to Hawaiians in U.S. life expectancy.

Opposite: The Hyland Lake Park Reserve is located barely more than a mile south of Interstate 494, one of the busiest stretches of freeway in the Twin Cities area. Hyland offers a close-in haven for walkers, joggers, bikers, skiers, and general all-around nature lovers. Consisting of more than 12,000 acres, Hyland includes the Richardson Nature Center, a ninety-acre lake, restored prairie lands, and a mixed hardwoods area, where you will find this wise old oak tree.

"There are few places in the world where you can live in a country setting surrounded by wheat fields, lovely wetlands, silence, and peace, and within a mere twenty-minute drive embrace the cultural delights of a sophisticated metropolitan area, such as the Minnesota Orchestra, Minneapolis Institute of Arts, Childrens Theatre, art galleries, and fine dining." **Sandy Bradley, Executive Search Consultant, Wells, Bradley & Assoc.**

Top: Four women practice their sculling technique on the Mississippi River. Although the season in the Twin Cities lasts only about six months, sculling and sweep rowing are quite popular. Between two hundred and three hundred hearty souls belong to one of two local clubs or are members of a college team.

Bottom: Touring the central Mississippi riverfront area of Minneapolis aboard the Anson Northrup excursion boat is popular warm-weather enter-tainment. The excursion boat offers narrated tours during the summer and is docked at Boom Island Park. The pros-perity of Minneapolis began not far downstream at St. Anthony Falls; now the area is rapidly being redeveloped into a major recreational and tourist attraction. So the river provides for Minneapolis again.

Opposite: The Mississippi River, viewed here from the Ford Parkway Bridge, flows through the Twin Cities almost silently, always there but rarely getting in the way. Perceptive and concerned Twin Citians are beginning to realize the old river was worked pretty hard over the years and now deserves a little care. Together with govern-ment organizations, they are working to protect the river and the river front.

"I love being able to walk from my front door to a lake edged with trees, where I can watch for migrating birds in fall and spring, keep track of growing ducklings in the summer, and watch lights flash on the frozen surface of ice in the winter. I also love being able to drive out of town and find myself in just over an hour below high wooded bluffs on the Mississippi below Red Wing. The Twin Cities have many urban pleasures, but I think I like best their proximity to accessible countryside." **Susan Allen Toth, Writer, Adjunct Professor at Macalester College**

Top inset: St. Paul's Como Park was named after Como, Italy, the birthplace of the man who originally farmed potatoes in the area. This fountain, named *Schiffman* after its donor, was fashioned after one seen in Italy in approximately 1898. It can be seen by the circular drive near the Pavilion.

Bottom inset: Since 1915, the Como Park Conservatory in St. Paul has been a refuge for the winter weary. The colors and scents and the moist warmth of the air fill your senses, and you always leave calmed and refreshed. Bring your children, your grandma, your camera, and enjoy.

Opposite: *Minnesota* in the Dakota language means "sky-tinted water," and this sunrise image of Lake Como in St. Paul surely says Minnesota. Como Park is one of St. Paul's oldest and most popular parks. The lake plays host to a small community of ducks, and many a family has introduced its young children to the pleasures of waterfowl watching on its banks.

"Having moved from Boston, I am delighted to find I am as close to water as I ever was on the coast. Minnesota — where mother nature proves she's alive and well." **Michael English, Architect, H & E Architects**

"Whether watching hawks soar overhead or Siberian tigers romping in the snow, Twin Citians are able to share the richness and value of wildlife in a wonderful urban setting. How fortunate for all of us!" **Kathryn R. Roberts, Ph.D., Director, Minnesota Zoo**

Above: Enjoying the leisure life, this gorilla twosome lives at the Como Park Zoo in St. Paul. Free to the public and surrounded by spacious park grounds, the Como Zoo has long been a favorite with Twin Cities families. It offers a schedule of special activities for children, and Sparky the Seal shows off some tricks several times a week.

Top left: Youngster meets youngster at the Minnesota Zoo in Apple Valley, about twenty-five minutes south of the center of either Minneapolis or St. Paul. Considered one of the finest zoos in the country, the Minnesota Zoo has special environments for Minnesota native species like beavers, owls, pumas, and wolverines. The zoo's new coral reef exhibit, with more than one hundred species of colorful tropical fish, provides fascinating underwater viewing. For some visitors, though, a tiny baby goat is excitement enough.

Bottom left: A family bikes the winding, up-and-down paths of St. Paul's Indian Mounds Park. The park affords excellent views of the Mississippi River and skyline. On the Fourth of July, Indian Mounds Park is a favorite place from which to watch fireworks over the State Capitol to the west.

Opposite: November frost decorates the forest floor in Crosby Farm Nature Area, a preserve adjacent to the Mississippi River in southwestern St. Paul. Winding asphalt paths and dirt trails (some made by resident deer) criss-cross the area, which contains pebble beaches and two lakes, home to muskrats, frogs, herons and other waterfowl.

Overleaf: The first snows of the season are sometimes the prettiest when the colors of fall still linger. An early November snow mixed two seasons at the Highland Golf Course in St. Paul.

"There is no place on earth which captures any better the changes in our four seasons than Minnesota. Perhaps the fall is the best example, when the leaves turn on their spectacular color show and contrast with Minnesota's 10,000-plus lakes and streams. It is a thing of beauty which only nature, using Minnesota as a stage, can produce and do it so well." **Curtis L. Carlson, Chairman & CEO, Carlson Companies, Inc.**

FACES & PLACES
Twin Cities Lifestyles

"*After traveling from one end of the globe to the other—and a few places in-between, I couldn't imagine a better place to live. With four very distinct seasons to experience allowing us no boredom, and people who understand adventure!*" **Ann Bancroft,**

Educator\Lecturer\Outdoor Leader

Opposite top: You can't fight winter in Minnesota—it returns every year. The best thing to do is don warm clothes—don't forget a hat—and hit the snow-covered hills with your sled. If you can get someone to go down the hill with you, all the better. Hold on tight, scream a little, and watch out for trees!

Opposite left: Excelsior, on Lake Minnetonka, was once a posh resort area "far to the west" of Minneapolis and St. Paul. One went for the day, or the summer for the luxury hotels, paddlewheel excursion boats, and a large amusement park. Today, Excelsior doesn't seem so far away, and its small-town personality, fresh air, and lakefront-living style attract many city commuters. This large shoreline park at the end of the main street offers geese, a swimming beach, a bandshell, and sailboat and sunset views.

Opposite center: Well known around the country for its nightly offerings of live jazz, the Dakota Bar & Grill in St. Paul's Bandana Square also serves up excellent meals. Shown here is a truly regional dish of Minnesota duckling roasted with blueberries, mint, and onions, served with wild rice. The Dakota specializes in foods and flavors of the Upper Midwest. Bandana Square, just south of Como Park, is also the present site of the Children's Museum.

Opposite right: In a setting rich with history, the American Indian Movement's annual Pow Wow is held in Fort Snelling State Park, where the Mississippi and Minnesota rivers meet. The three-day Pow Wow, held over Labor Day weekend, includes daily dance competitions that draw between three hundred and four hundred Native American dancers from all over the United States and Canada. All tribal nations are welcome to the gathering, and over 15,000 visitors attend.

Above: St. Paul has attracted a large number of Hmong refugees from northern Laos, and in fact may have the second largest Hmong population in the United States. Many of the women have become involved in business by selling their needlework through the Hmong Handwork Shop on Grand Avenue in St. Paul. The shop has achieved a national reputation for the fine quality and large selection of Hmong textile art it carries. Employee Lucy Vang holds some cross-stitch work by Lao Thor, her grandmother.

Above: Throughout Minnesota, the fall season is savored and the colors are photographed endlessly. Many streets in the Twin Cities become tunnels of red, yellow, and orange, bringing a glow to everything. As joggers, walkers, and bikers move along Mississippi River Boulevard in St. Paul, they see many small still lifes like this one.

Top inset: A pretty trendy place to shop, eat, or just stroll these days is Grand Avenue in St. Paul, where you'll find this Creative Kidstuff store. Originally a streetcar corridor along which businesses located to serve the neighborhoods, Grand Avenue is now chock full of specialty shops and restaurants, several operating from beautiful old homes. Here's the street to find Minnesota T-shirts, Minnesota books, and Minnesota cheese, right along with Mexican clothing, an Irish mug, and a Vietnamese meal. Grand Avenue runs from the west end of the downtown area almost to the Mississippi River.

Center inset: This attractive townhouse complex at the corner of Laurel Avenue and Nina Street in St. Paul served as home to a young F. Scott Fitzgerald and his parents, though not under the best of circumstances. Fitzgerald's father lost his job as a salesman in Buffalo, New York, in 1908 and the family returned to St. Paul and moved in with Mrs. Fitzgerald's wealthy mother, the widow McQuillan. Fitzgerald's father never worked again and the family lived off the widow's fortune. The complex was built in 1884 of brownstone and red pressed brick.

Bottom inset: In a scene that probably has taken place every spring for many years, two young girls collect blossoms for their hair in Irvine Park. One of the city's earliest residential neighborhoods, Irvine Park still has more pre–Civil War homes than any neighborhood in St. Paul. Saved by inclusion on the National Register of Historic Places, the restored park residences include the 1872 home of Minnesota Territory's first governor, Alexander Ramsey. Many of the homes face onto a small square with trees, benches, and a graceful fountain. Supposedly the original fountain was a good place for the local Tom Sawyers to store their catches from a day of river fishing.

Top left: A curler delivers a stone down the ice to the waiting brooms of sweepers at the St. Paul Curling Club. Curling was established in St. Paul in 1885, but its origins go back to Scotland, where it has been played for over three hundred years. Originally, curling at the club was a sport of the upper class. Today curling is open to everyone, and the St. Paul Curling Club is a family-friendly place to spend some winter days and try your luck at this unique sport. And there's no wind-chill factor!

Top center: Some Minnesotans love winter; some tolerate it. But they all know how to cope with it, and that includes many layers of clothing, hats, mittens, and boots. This young lady peers out from her cocoon of warmth during St. Paul's Winter Carnival, an almost-annual event since 1938, although it actually began in 1885. She's set to enjoy a chilly ride during the carnival's Sleigh and Cutter Parade in Como Park.

Top right: German-speaking peoples constituted the largest single foreign-born group in Minnesota from 1860 until 1905. One group that works to preserve the German culture is the Volksfest Association of Minnesota, located at 301 Summit Avenue in the Volksfest Kulturhaus. A good way to experience all things German is to attend the association's annual Deutscher Tag (German Day), held the second Sunday in June. Here, folk dancer Bob Hanson is shown in the Ratskeller of the Kulturhaus where members hold monthly dinners and meetings. A few special dinners are open to the public as well, with authentic German cooking to be sure.

Right: Germans have long had an affinity for beer and were skilled brewers. At one point in 1878, Germans held fifty-four of St. Paul's fifty-seven brewer's licenses. Twin Citians appreciate good beer, and they've quickly taken to those from the Summit Brewing Company. A small "craft" brewery, Summit produces a variety of fresh beers in this brewing tank in a vintage 1938 brewhouse on University Avenue. Tours are available.

Opposite: A restored Queen Anne style home, circa 1891, on St. Paul's Summit Avenue is one of many such elegant residences along the avenue's four and one-half miles of history, probably the best-preserved American example of the Victorian monumental residential boulevard. As Oliver Towne wrote in his charming book *Saint Paul is my beat,* "Were St. Paul likened to a tree, Summit would be its trunk; personify the city and Summit is the main artery, from which life flowed into the counting houses, the business marts."

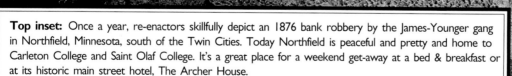

Top inset: Once a year, re-enactors skillfully depict an 1876 bank robbery by the James-Younger gang in Northfield, Minnesota, south of the Twin Cities. Today Northfield is peaceful and pretty and home to Carleton College and Saint Olaf College. It's a great place for a weekend get-away at a bed & breakfast or at its historic main street hotel, The Archer House.

Bottom inset: Drive east from St. Paul about twenty minutes and you will find Stillwater, a New England–looking town perched on the banks of the St. Croix, a National Wild and Scenic River. Founded in 1843, before Minnesota became a territory in 1848, Stillwater was the valley's major logging and milling center, being efficiently located between extensive pine forests for supply and a rushing river for transportation. Much of the late–nineteenth-century architecture of Stillwater remains.

Right: A rocky canyon called the Dalles of the Saint Croix River near the 1850s logging town of Taylors Falls. A tributary of the Mississippi, the 140-mile St. Croix was one of the first-designated National Wild and Scenic Rivers. The Upper St. Croix runs rapidly through pine and hardwood forests, while the Lower St. Croix is broad and shallow and passes state parks and river towns. You can board an excursion boat at Taylors Falls or rent a canoe at one of several points along the river.

Top inset: The St. Paul Saints play under the stars at Municipal Stadium to an enthusiastic crowd that likes baseball *outside*. Twin Citians have always had a love affair with baseball, and the original Saints were a major fixture in St. Paul, playing from 1901 until 1956.

Bottom inset: Minnesotans love to read, and they actively support the literary community. Book readings by national and local authors take place at the many fine bookstores in the Twin Cities several times a week, and they are well attended. Here, author Carl Hiassen reads from his novel *Strip Tease* at the Hungry Mind Bookstore in St. Paul. Locally owned, one-of-a-kind, and bursting with wonderful literature, the Hungry Mind is located on Grand Avenue, on the edge of the Macalaster College campus.

Right: Red barns and corn fields, like this winter scene near Afton, Minnesota (southeast of St. Paul), are a familiar sight to Minnesotans. In fact, red barns are as much a part of Minnesota's landscape as its rivers and woods. Minnesota is among the top half-dozen agricultural states in the nation, and corn is the number one crop in Minnesota, thanks in large part to hybrids developed to suit Minnesota's climate.

Top: Old-fashioned sleigh rides can still be found in the tiny village of Copas, northeast of St. Paul along the St. Croix River. The very first Swedish immigrants to Minnesota country settled not far from here in 1850, and you can still find fine Swedish-American cooking at Crabtree's Kitchen, a homey restaurant you can't miss in a town so small you'll almost drive right by it!

Bottom: A favorite weekend drive from the Twin Cities takes you to the southeast, through Mississippi River bluff country called the Hiawatha Valley. Red Wing, shown here, prospered in the nineteenth century, specializing in leather processing, lime quarrying, and clay-related industries. Many a Minnesotan has a prized pottery jug or bowl stamped "Red Wing," and more than a few feet sport Red Wing boots or shoes.

Opposite: Fall in Minnesota definitely means colored leaves, but fall also means apples. Fresh apples, crunchy and tart or sweet, depending on your preference. Apple pie, strudel, muffins, cider. A Twin Cities favorite "apple excursion" is to Aamodt's Apple Farm in Stillwater, east of St. Paul. Offering more than twenty-four varieties, the Aamodt family has been running the business for many generations, and their apples' quality is among the highest.

"I love how we pride ourselves on thriving in a harsh climate. Minnesotans always have. Way back in 1873, the St. Paul Daily Pioneer *reported the case of a New England woman who was so weak she couldn't sweep her own room. But in less than a year after moving here, 'she chased her husband a mile and a quarter with a pitchfork, and gave birth to a pair of twins the same afternoon.'"* **Peg Meier, Author**

Above: Minneapolis got its beginnings in the tiny town of St. Anthony, officially incorporated in 1855, but developed for grist and lumber milling in the 1820s initially by soldiers from nearby Fort Snelling. A wonderful place to experience what was St. Anthony is Pracna on Main Historic Restaurant, housed in a restored building that has served as a "dining saloon" since 1890. Pictures of the building's past adorn the walls, and the streets out front are cobblestone. Just across the street is the Mississippi River, with paths and parks for pleasant after-dinner strolling or sunset watching.

Opposite top: Members of the Grace Community Church Gospel Choir raise their voices to heaven at an outdoor concert in St. Paul's Phalen Park. Grace is the best known and most active African-American congregation on St. Paul's East Side.

Opposite, bottom left: The art of Polish paper-cutting is demonstrated during the Christmas holidays at Murphy's Landing, an eighty-seven-acre outdoor living history museum located in the small Minnesota River town of Shakopee, southwest of Minneapolis. Several buildings have been reassembled on the site to depict frontier life between 1840 and 1890. The settlement of Poles in Minnesota started just before the Civil War, with strong settlement in rural areas to pursue a life of farming.

Opposite, bottom right: A young girl shares a moment with her grandfather, a member of I Ballerini di Minnesota, during an outdoor performance at Lake Phalen in St. Paul. The troupe of Italian dancers was founded in 1970 and performs throughout the year.

Top inset: Twin Cities' summers are very pleasant, with an average July temperature of 74 degrees. And with all the lakes we have, it doesn't take long to get to one, cast a line, and enjoy the sunset, like this family at Lake Hiawatha, just north of Lake Nokomis in south Minneapolis.

Center inset: Conversation and a meal under the summer sky is a favorite pastime for Twin Citians. With a fairly short warm weather season, residents never get enough of the outdoors. This small cafe is near the West Bank campus of the University of Minnesota in an area known as Seven Corners (yes, there are). The area has gone through many phases: Scandinavian immigrant enclave, down-and-out skid row, sixties student radicals' hangout, and now, an area of small theaters and diverse restaurants favored by students and professionals alike.

Bottom inset: The largest body of water in the Twin Cities area is Lake Minnetonka, long a haven for the boating crowd. Located west of Minneapolis, Lake Minnetonka is bounded by a number of well-tuned suburbs, many considered quite prestigious addresses. All that boating on the lake can make you hungry, and a favorite spot to tie up is Lord Fletcher's in Spring Park. There's indoor and deck dining with a great view of the lake.

Opposite: One of the nicest things about living in the Twin Cities is the fact you can be "out of town" in about thirty minutes from just about anywhere. Watching a sunset over Eagle Lake, near Carver County's Baylor Regional Park (southwest of the Metro), is surely worth the short drive. The Suburban Hennepin Regional Park District includes 25,000 acres of such close-in parks and preserves for your personal pleasure.

"Though my work takes me to many places, I know that I am home when I return to my roots in Minnesota. The beauties of the North Shore and the St. Croix relax me and rest my soul; the tremendous variety and quality of arts and cultural organizations enlarge my spirit; educational institutions and public debate over issues and policy constantly challenge my mind and energies."
Anita M. Pampusch, President, College of St. Catherine

Above: When you live in the Twin Cities and you want to plant a tree or a shrub or a flower garden, you head for the University of Minnesota Landscape Arboretum. Located southwest of Minneapolis in Chanhassen, the arboretum offers living examples of what will grow in Minnesota and how it will look, a wonderful reference library, a bright and sunny cafeteria, a small gift shop full of unique items, and 905 acres of rolling hills, woods, and formal gardens. In spring, these flowering crab trees and dandelions are a sight for sore eyes for winter-white-weary Minnesotans.

Top inset: The place to be if you really like to dance nonstop is Glam Slam Dance Club in the downtown Minneapolis warehouse district. A well-run endeavor of the pop star (and Twin Cities native) commonly called Prince, Glam Slam has a million-dollar light show playing over its 13,000-square-foot dance floor, a dazzling piece of techno-wonder. "Funk Night," shown here, and Saturday night are the most popular evenings, drawing up to 1,500 bodies ready to sweat it out on the dance floor. Another enterprise of Prince's, Paisley Park Studios in Chanhassen, puts the Twin Cities on the map of the music-making world.

Center inset: The legalization of gaming casinos has created a business bonanza for Native Americans in Minnesota. Mystic Lake, in Prior Lake, is one of the state's largest casinos, running twenty-four hours a day, seven days a week. A short drive south of the Twin Cities in the Minnesota River valley, Mystic Lake Casino is 135,000 square feet of slot machines (there are one thousand), blackjack tables, a huge bingo amphitheater, keno games, and an excellent restaurant.

Bottom inset: This street of rowhouses on Milwaukee Avenue (south of downtown Minneapolis) was occupied at the turn-of-the-century by working-class families, many employed at the nearby rail yards. The homes have been preserved as private residences, and the street offers a taste of the past. Like other types of businesses, the railroads offered employment to many immigrants by advertising in Europe, so great was the expansion of rail transportation in Minnesota.

Above: If life has been a little too dull for you lately, jump in your car and head for Valleyfair, a sixty-eight–acre amusement park in Shakopee, southwest of the metro. Satisfy your need for speed on the Corkscrew, a hair-raising ride that climbs and drops and loops and—all at fifty miles per hour. After you've recovered, there's a lot more rides to try and special areas for the very young. There's great food and entertainment, too.

Left: A young man shows off his break-dancing skills at the Minneapolis Institute of Arts's Rose Fete, an event that celebrates a variety of art forms. The institute was built on the site of the former rose garden of Villa Rosa, an estate belonging to the city's first mayor, Dorilus Morrison.

Bottom left: A young boy feeds the horses after a hard day on the Camp Courage Wagon Train trail. Camp Courage is the summer camp arm of Courage Center, a facility in Golden Valley that provides rehabilitation and independent living skills to people with physical disabilities and sensory impairments. The eight-day wagon train annually raises close to $90,000 and numbers about 250 people, fifty wagons, and lots of horses.

Opposite: Winter ice encloses bottomland hardwoods in Louisville Swamp, part of the Minnesota Valley National Wildlife Refuge near Shakopee. Located along a seventy-two-mile stretch of the Minnesota River, the valley includes numerous recreation areas and trails. Carved out by the glacial River Warren 11,000 years ago, the valley is a rich environment for plants, waterfowl, and wildlife.

"Cityscapes and outdoor spaces do not clash, they mesh, such as the magnificent way the Mississippi River winds through the Cities." **David Winfield, Professional Baseball Player for the Minnesota Twins, and Columnist for the St. Paul Pioneer Press**

LANDMARKS & LYRICS
Music, History, and Art in the Twin Cities

"*Where else can you spend the day studying wolf tracks left in pristine wilderness to the north, and attend a magnificent concert, opera, or play that same evening? This mix, plus the people it attracts, makes the Twin Cities a vibrant environment in which to live one's own life to the fullest.*" **L. David Mech, Wildlife Research Biologist, North Central Forest Experiment Station**

Opposite top: If you think it takes you a long time to complete a project around the house, consider this: The interior of the Cathedral of St. Paul was not considered "finished" until 1953, although the first service was held in 1915! The neobaroque interior can seat about three thousand and is noted for the number and beauty of its chapels, which are dedicated to the patron saints of the various nations whose people settled St. Paul.

Opposite left: A member of the Happy Wanderers German Band entertains a polka-happy crowd during the Minnesota Orchestra's annual Viennese Sommerfest, a three-week, midsummer event held in Peavey Plaza on the Nicollet Mall, adjacent to Orchestra Hall. A variety of music is performed in the evening, and tasty treats and beverages are available as well. Large numbers of German-speaking immigrants came to the Twin Cities area, and music played a central role in many early German-American associations. The oldest was the Turnverein, a society founded in 1857; by 1920, there were more than fifty such groups.

Opposite center: The Twin Cities is well known for its excellent theaters, and much of that reputation has its roots in the Guthrie Theater in Minneapolis. This North American repertory theater was a dream come true for the great Irish actor and director, Sir Tyrone Guthrie, and it was made possible by the same civic leaders and families of wealth who have contributed so much to the building of Minneapolis and its cultural community. Guthrie directed the first production, "Hamlet," in 1963. The theater presents a broad array of nationally acclaimed productions from classical masterpieces to contemporary American and foreign works.

Opposite right: Not a bad seat exists in the Guthrie Theater due to its thrust stage, modeled after Canada's Stratford Festival Theater, enabling actors to play to an audience that semicircles them. A member of the resident repertory theater is shown performing Alexander Ostrovsky's "Too Clever by Half," a classic Russian satire written in 1868.

Above: Minnesota's State Capitol building against a twilight sky. Rising slightly above downtown St. Paul, the Capitol is considered an excellent example of Roman Renaissance architecture. Young architect Cass Gilbert, whose career in St. Paul had been off to a slow start, entered a competition for the design of the Capitol and won. His career blossomed, and he went on to become one of the important transitional architects of America. An interesting detail of the Capitol's exterior is the quadriga and six statues above the main entrance, the work of sculptor Daniel Chester French. The virtues represented are Wisdom, Courage, Bounty, Truth, Integrity, and Prudence, noble ones indeed.

Opposite: The inside of the Minnesota State Capitol in St. Paul is as beautiful and ornate as the outside. The building was completed in 1904 for the magnificent sum of $4.5 million. It is great fun to explore the interior, which incorporates more than twenty kinds of marble and several types of Minnesota stone, and to find little gems like this doorway and floor design. Free tours are given throughout the week; guides will teach you lots of interesting facts about the Capitol.

Opposite, inset: *Monument to the Living,* a statue created by Rodger Brodin in memory of all living American veterans, is shown superimposed on the Minnesota Vietnam Veterans Memorial. The memorial was thoughtfully designed and includes many interesting details. The floor of the memorial's plaza, in the shape of the state, contains 68,000 square grids representing the number of Minnesotans who served in Vietnam, with darker squares indicating the hometowns of those killed or missing. A granite wall is inscribed with the names of those 1,120 individuals. Minnesota limestone and native greenery surround the area. Both the statue and memorial can be found between the State Capitol and Veterans Service Building, just north of downtown St. Paul.

Top: Two young visitors from Iowa investigate the tornado machine in the Experiment Gallery at the Science Museum of Minnesota. Located in downtown St. Paul, the Science Museum provides a hands-on educational environment that is fun, well laid-out, and made-to-order for kids who prefer to be moving while they're learning. There are dinosaur exhibits and labs, a Hall of Anthropology with an Egyptian mummy, a family of stuffed polar bears, an exhibit explaining Minnesota's landscape, and the hold-on-to-your-seat Omnitheater with its domed screen wrapping around you. It's a place to educate even your most rambunctious child.

Bottom: Although the tenor of Garrison Keillor's "A Prairie Home Companion" radio show is back-porch country, it is broadcast from this elegant building, the World Theater, in downtown St. Paul. Opened in 1910 as the Sam S. Schubert Theater, the building's interior is rich with gilded ornamentation and old world charm. Rising behind the theater in this photo is the World Trade Center, a meeting and resource center devoted to exploring and increasing international trade.

"From the Minnesota Orchestra to Como Park, the Minneapolis Sculpture Garden and Penumbra Theatre to our wonderful new History Center, there is something here for everyone everyday. Where else could you visit a 19th-century working farm, a Victorian mansion, an 1827 fort, discover the traditions of wild ricing, research your house history, and see Prince's 'Purple Rain' costume in just one day?" **Nina Archabal, Director, Minnesota Historical Society**

Opposite: The Cathedral of St. Paul bears witness to the zeal and devotion to a cause of one man — John Ireland. His cause, Catholic immigration to Minnesota, resulted in St. Paul becoming a city rich with parish neighborhoods, strong family ties, and civic pride. An Irish immigrant who never forgot the starving peasants of his homeland, John Ireland, who ascended to Archbishop during his lifetime, was responsible for giving many of his country-people a new start in Minnesota. The Cathedral, located at the east end of Selby Avenue, is one of the largest church buildings in North America and was built to resemble Michelangelo's St. Peter's in Rome. It is open to the public every day.

Top: The name James J. Hill looms large in St. Paul history. Hill was a Canadian immigrant of meager means who rose from a freight clerk on the St. Paul levee to become one of the nation's most successful railroad men. The James J. Hill Home, which attests to the wealth Hill achieved, is on Summit Avenue and is open to the public. Completed in 1891, the house has 36,000 square feet, thirty-two rooms, and thirteen bathrooms (well, the family did raise eight children here). Despite its size, the home is surprisingly devoid of overly elaborate details. It is said the Hill home reflects the independence, practicality, and rugged personality of its master. As Carol Brink notes in her book *The Twin Cities,* "Jim Hill had lost an eye in an early accident with an arrow. . . . He still had two inner eyes, one for the vast dream and another one for the main chance, and . . . some instinct for greatness made him combine the dream with the reality to build an empire."

Center: The front entrance of the Minnesota Governor's Residence on St. Paul's historic Summit Avenue. Built in 1910 by lumber baron Horace Hills Irvine, the home was given to the state in 1965. Governor Karl Rolvaag and his family were the first official residents, and their first guest was Crown Prince Harald of Norway.

Bottom: Home to the Minnesota Territory's first governor, the Alexander Ramsey House today is open to the public and is filled with Victorian furnishings and personal family mementos. Located in the historic Irvine Park neighborhood, just a few blocks southwest of downtown St. Paul, the home was constructed of native limestone between 1868 and 1872. Ramsey's granddaughters lived in the home until 1964.

Above: Viewed through a window of the Ordway Theater, St. Paul's Landmark Center rises above Rice Park in downtown. Once a federal courts building, post office, and customs clearing house, the Landmark Center is now a cultural center. An exuberant collection of turrets, towers, and gables on the outside, the Landmark Center has an interior that is equally fascinating. It has been well preserved, but not "slicked up," and a very distinct aura of the past lingers on. St. Paul was a haven for mobsters in the twenties and thirties, and the courtrooms you can visit here once saw the likes of Ma Barker, John Dillinger, and Alvin "Creepy" Karpis (personally escorted by J. Edgar Hoover). The building is open every day, and there is a small cafe on the first floor.

Opposite, left inset: The well-respected Minnesota Museum of American Art on St. Peter Street in downtown St. Paul is committed to art that reflects the cultural diversity of this country. Temporary exhibitions are shown at the Landmark Center, located a few blocks away. Admission is free, and the museum is open six days a week.

Top inset: The elegant Main Hall of the Ordway Music Theatre in downtown St. Paul offers unrestricted viewing from over 1,800 seats. Described by *Time* magazine as "one of the handsomest public spaces for music in America," the Ordway serves as the principal performing space for the Minnesota Opera, the Saint Paul Chamber Orchestra, and the Schubert Club. The architect's description of the building's design, "classical and yet irregular," could describe the Ordway's offerings as well: jazz, ballet, Broadway shows, popular music, ethnic dance, and family entertainment.

Bottom inset: The Twin Cities are blessed with the only full-time chamber orchestra in the United States, the Saint Paul Chamber Orchestra, shown here performing at the Ordway Music Theatre. Delighting audiences for more than thirty-four years, the orchestra annually presents more than one hundred concerts in several venues in the Twin Cities. The Saint Paul Chamber Orchestra presents bold, innovative interpretations of many eras, from Baroque to contemporary minimalist works.

MINNESOTA MUSEUM OF ART

Top: Zebulon Pike was an explorer appointed by Thomas Jefferson, who wished to establish strong American authority over the vast territory he had acquired with the 1803 Louisiana Purchase. Pike found a strategic military site at the confluence of the Minnesota and Mississippi rivers, and the first military post in this region was Fort Snelling, first called Fort St. Anthony and built in the 1820s. Much of the fort has been restored to its original appearance, and living history re-enactors, like this young piper, give visitors a taste of fort living. The fort is open daily through the warm weather months, and several special events are held on weekends.

Center: The Henry H. Sibley House is located in the village of Mendota, the first permanent white settlement in what became Minnesota, located just south of St. Paul on the Minnesota River. The 1835 home, open for tours, is the oldest existing private home in the state and is a well-preserved example of early limestone construction. Mr. Sibley, who began his career in Minnesota managing a fur trade company, obviously was a man ahead of his time. He was a bachelor for many years, and he reportedly made his own pickles, washed his own dishes, and milked his own cows! An outside stairway on his house led to the attic, which was always available to Native Americans who needed shelter.

Bottom: With a long and colorful history, it is only fitting that Minnesota should have a worthy place to tell and preserve her stories, visually and verbally. That place is the Minnesota History Center, a dramatic building overlooking downtown St. Paul on Kellogg Boulevard. A user-friendly, spacious, and airy place, the Minnesota History Center includes a full floor of visual exhibits, a comprehensive research center, classrooms for special programs, two Minnesota-theme gift stores, and a lovely cafeteria. An extra bonus is a stunning view of the State Capitol.

Opposite: With commercial airplanes roaring overhead from the Minneapolis–St. Paul International Airport, these American lotus lilies serenely float upon the waters of Snelling Lake in Fort Snelling State Park. The lotus lily is Minnesota's largest wildflower, with blossoms being six to ten inches across and a leaf blade width of up to two feet. The Native Americans used both the seeds and starchy rootstalks for food.

Right: This is probably Minnesota's most beautiful fish. The sculpture, titled *Standing Glass Fish,* was created by Frank Gehry of wood, glass, steel, and silicone. You can find it in the Sage and John Cowles Conservatory, part of the Minneapolis Sculpture Garden. The seven-and-one-half-acre urban garden is located next to the Walker Art Museum and Guthrie Theater and contains some forty sculptures by leading American and international artists.

Below: The fountain sculpture *Spoonbridge and Cherry* creates lovely reflections in the small pond nearly surrounding it. An important element in the Minneapolis Sculpture Garden, the piece is twenty-nine feet high and fifty-two feet long and was created by Claes Oldenburg and Coosje van Bruggen. Downtown Minneapolis, seen in the background, can be reached by car or by taking the nearby Irene Hixon Whitney footbridge into Loring Park. The Sculpture Garden is free and open year-round.

"The Twin Cities can boast of two major orchestra and a host of semi-professional ones; more than thirty theater companies; a large chamber music pool of players and an enthusiastic audience for these more intimate concerts; a burgeoning dance community; and lots more. The Twin Cites is the place to be for the arts!" **Philip Brunelle, Artistic Director and Founder, Plymouth Music Series of Minnesota**

Top: The Minnesota Orchestra, conducted by Edo de Waart, performs Carmina Burana at Orchestra Hall in Minneapolis. Known throughout the world, the Minnesota Orchestra presents a fifty-two-week season to appreciative audiences. The orchestra evolved from the Minneapolis Symphony Orchestra, which gave its first performances in 1903 under the direction of Emil Oberhoffer, a German immigrant.

Center: The characters in The Children's Theater Company presentation of "The Wonderful Wizard of Oz" are well-loved figures: Dorothy and her little dog Toto, the farmyard Scarecrow, the creaky Tin Woodsman, and the Cowardly Lion. The children in all of us are lucky indeed to have the nation's second-largest theater for young audiences here in Minneapolis. When the lights go down in the much-lauded venue, classic children's literature comes to life in lively and colorful adaptations that sweep you away to other places and other times.

Bottom: The interior of the Historic State Theatre in Minneapolis, beautifully renovated to make its Italian Renaissance details gleam. First open in 1921 as a vaudeville house, and used for a variety of purposes since, the State now plays host to first-class national and local performances. Come early so you have time to appreciate the elegant surroundings.

"The Historic State Theatre is like a precious jewel or beautiful keepsake from days gone by. I shudder to think how close we came to losing this remarkable piece of Minneapolis history. It is a living, breathing example of how crucial the arts are to any culture. Ask anyone, 'Who owns the theatre?' People generally respond, 'We do. The citizens of Minneapolis.'" **Sharon Sayles Belton, Mayor, City of Minneapolis**

Top inset: A tour of the American Swedish Institute in Minneapolis starts in the African mahogany–paneled Grand Hall. Housed in the former mansion of successful Swedish immigrant Swan Turnblad, the Institute has over fifteen rooms open to the public and numerous Swedish exhibits.

Bottom inset: Interior of the Basilica of Saint Mary, at the western edge of downtown Minneapolis. The Basilica is on the National Register of Historic Places and in 1926 became the first such church in the United States to be proclaimed a basilica. Designed by French architect Emmanuel Louis Masqueray, the Basilica seats 1,600 below an impressive dome that rises two hundred feet above floor level. Tours are available.

Right: On a hot summer day, father and son lie on the cool stone of Peavey Plaza in downtown Minneapolis. Peavey Plaza is located right on Nicollet Mall, adjacent to modern Orchestra Hall. After a stroll up and down the Mall, the plaza provides a peaceful place to feed the ducks or to feed yourself an ice cream cone. In the winter, the pool serves as an ice skating rink, surrounded by the twinkling lights of the city skyline.

Opposite: The past is revisited as melodramas are performed on the stage of the University of Minnesota Showboat. Permanently moored on the east bank of the Mississippi River, this elegant craft was constructed in 1898 and sailed under General John Newton.

Top: A partial view of the Minneapolis Institute of Arts, a beaux arts style building first opened in 1915. With a comprehensive collection of more than 80,000 objects, the MIA is recognized as one of the great museums in America, and admission is free for most exhibits. Three floors of galleries and eight curatorial departments represent the history of art from 25,000 B.C. to the present, and include paintings, prints, drawings, decorative arts, sculpture, textiles, and photography. However, it took a while to create such a collection. In "Landmarks—Old and New" by Lael Berman, it is noted "For the 1915 grand opening, art from the private collection of James J. Hill was brought by horse and wagon from the railroad baron's St. Paul mansion to help fill the walls."

Center: A college campus often is a world unto itself, isolated from its surroundings. Not so the University of Minnesota, located in the heart of the Twin Cities and bounded by established business, industrial, and residential neighborhoods and the Mississippi River. This very urban institution provides outstanding educational opportunities on a sprawling campus dating back to a federal land grant of 1851 (later opening its doors as the University in 1869). Over the years, the University has gained a reputation as a first-rate research facility, especially in the fields of medicine, engineering, and super-computing.

Bottom: A shiny new addition to the University of Minnesota's East Bank campus is the stainless-steel–clad Frederick R. Weisman Art Museum. Designed by architect Frank Gehry, the multi-million–dollar facility has 11,000 square feet of exhibition space to house work from the institution's impressive collection. The Weisman will also offer students lectures and symposia.

CELEBRATING THE TWIN CITIES
Festivals and Fairs

"*The Twin Cities is one metropolitan area which has not lost its soul.*

There is a depth and richness to living here — from lakes used by all

the people to the great cultural institutions, spiritual organizations,

health care innovation, and an attitude of supporting and helping

others — which enriches and ennobles the quality of life."

Bill George, President & CEO, Medtronic

Opposite top: The Minnesota Renaissance Festival, an annual event held south of Shakopee, includes seven stages offering continuous entertainment—magic acts and minstrels, comedians and mimes, court jesters and jugglers. Here, visitors enjoy zany humor on the Legend Stage. Costumed "wanderers" roam the grounds as well, looking for visitors from the twentieth century. They'll engage you in light-hearted banter, hoping to coax out a good laugh or silly grin.

Opposite left: Martina Masaquiza, with her son Gabriel, prepares a display of woven work from her native Ecuador at the Minnesota Crafts Festival, a juried event held each summer on the grounds of the College of St. Catherine in St. Paul.

Opposite center: Competition for the best apples at the Minnesota State Fair, a twelve-day, end-of-the-summer event. The fair got its start in the mid-1850s as a harvest event celebrating the agricultural bounty of Minnesota and the many practical skills of its citizens. Those skills are still applauded, and many serious apple growers will be asking a lot of questions at the fair, hoping to take home a ribbon next year.

Opposite right: If you're in St. Paul on the Fourth of July weekend, forget the diet and head down to the Taste of Minnesota festival on the grounds of the State Capitol. A four-day event, with lots of music, kids' rides, and fireworks every night, the Taste of Minnesota is really about food. More than thirty-five restaurants set up tents to serve mouth-watering goodies, like the ribs shown here from the Smokehouse B-B-Q Restaurant.

Above: Accordion player at the Svenskarnas Dag festival in Minnehaha Park, an annual event no self-respecting Minnesota Swede would want to miss. More immigrating Swedes made their home in Minnesota than in any other state, having arrived as early as 1850. Today, both in the United States and abroad, Minnesota is perceived as the most Swedish state in the union. Yah sure!

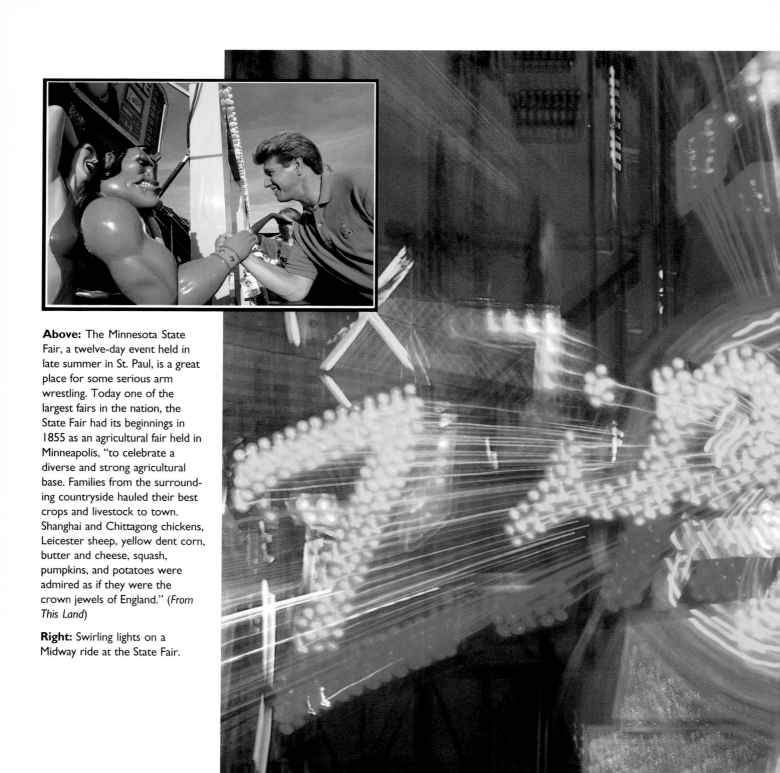

Above: The Minnesota State Fair, a twelve-day event held in late summer in St. Paul, is a great place for some serious arm wrestling. Today one of the largest fairs in the nation, the State Fair had its beginnings in 1855 as an agricultural fair held in Minneapolis, "to celebrate a diverse and strong agricultural base. Families from the surrounding countryside hauled their best crops and livestock to town. Shanghai and Chittagong chickens, Leicester sheep, yellow dent corn, butter and cheese, squash, pumpkins, and potatoes were admired as if they were the crown jewels of England." (*From This Land*)

Right: Swirling lights on a Midway ride at the State Fair.

"One of the things that I like best about the Twin Cities is that they are a unique combination of big-city living with small-town warmth and friendliness. The Twin Cities are the embodiment of wholesome, down-to-earth midwestern values combined with the rich, diverse social and cultural life of a big city. Twin Cities residents are the friendliest, most good-natured people that you will ever meet in any big city." **Kelly Ryan, Secretary, Department of Surgery, University of Minnesota**

Top inset: Ask Minnesotans what the State Fair means to them, and you'll get a lot of answers involving food. Freshly made Pronto Pups (elsewhere called corn dogs), slathered with mustard or ketchup or both, are a favorite of many fairgoers. Between snacks, you can test your hand-to-eye coordination at the midway games, try a tractor seat out for size on Machinery Hill, ooh and aah at the horse show, or see a national recording artist at the Grandstand, under the stars.

Bottom inset: The Twin Cities is home to a wide variety of nationalities, and nowhere is that more evident than in its selection of ethnic restaurants. A good way to get a sampling of the foods of many cultures is to attend St. Paul's Taste of Minnesota event. Here a young cook stirs a batch of shrimp fried rice at the Nankin Restaurant tent.

Top inset: On a sunny winter day, a couple enjoys ice sledding on frozen Lake Como during St. Paul's annual Winter Carnival. The oldest winter celebration in the country (the first was in 1886), the Winter Carnival is two weeks of indoor and outdoor fun, including the Torchlight and Grande Day Parades, sporting competitions, and the notorious red-caped Vulcans clanging up and down the streets of St. Paul in their finely restored fire engines. It's St. Paul's way of snubbing its nose at Old Man Winter.

Bottom inset: An evening visit to Rice Park in downtown St. Paul during Winter Carnival offers the results of an ice carving contest held the day before. Participants in the contest spend hours creating well-formed sculptures finished with intricate details. Art that melts must be seen as soon as possible, as a "winter thaw" day can alter the creator's intent in unusual ways.

One of St. Paul's claims to fame is its almost-annual Winter Carnival and the dramatic ice palaces that often accompany it. During the 1992 Winter Carnival, the height of the palace (150 feet) qualified it as the world's largest ice structure. St. Paulites did almost as well in 1888, when the ice palace reached 144 feet. More than 20,000 blocks of ice were needed then, most being cut from Lake Como. Winter can make you do crazy things in Minnesota!

Right: A member of the Minneapolis Aqua Jesters keeps kids smiling during the annual Summer Aquatennial Grande Day Parade in downtown Minneapolis, one of over seventy-five events scheduled during the ten-day celebration.

Below: The Minneapolis Aquatennial is a midsummer event celebrating the city's lakes, parks, and rivers. The triathlon competition shown here is a chance to test your mettle against hundreds of others as you swim, bike, and run in the Lake Nokomis area. As you can see, it's a little crowded at the beginning of this event!

"Being a recent resident, I'm sure there are many Twin Cities treasures I've yet to unearth. However, I have discovered great fishing spots, many cultural and sporting events, and best of all, the friendly, generous, hard-working people that are truly the Twin Cities' greatest asset."
Dennis Green, Head Football Coach, Minnesota Vikings

Left: The Uptown neighborhood of Minneapolis, loosely spreading out from the intersection of Lake Street and Hennepin Avenue, is an area where nothing is too unusual or too new. It attracts young professionals who like variety in their lives, interesting places to shop and eat, and lakes to skate around. The area's annual Uptown Art Fair draws more than five hundred artists and up to 300,000 visitors, making it most likely the Midwest's largest juried art show. Kids even get a chance to create their own masterpieces at the Kids Tent.

Top inset: At the Uptown Art Fair you'll probably find something you don't really need but that you want anyway, like these queenly clothes.

Bottom inset: Mom and daughter have fun shopping at Jan Shafer's Hattitudes booth, one of more than one hundred exhibits at the Minnesota Crafts Festival. Held every summer on the grounds of the College of St. Catherine, the two-day juried event features artists in a number of media with work for sale.

"I challenge anyone to find an environment which better fosters the often difficult, but truly harmonious, balance between one's devotion to commerce and one's interests in family, education, religion, society and the arts." **James D'Aquila, Managing Director, Dain Bosworth, Inc.**

Left: Svenskarnas Dag is the most important Swedish celebration in the Twin Cities, an area with a considerable number of residents descended from Swedish immigrants. Held in Minnehaha Park in south Minneapolis since 1933, the event attracts thousands who want to retain contact with the Swedish culture. There are dancers and singing groups, like the Svenskarnas Dag Girls Choir shown here, and much visiting with old friends over steaming cups of coffee.

Below: A proud Irishman leads his group through the streets of downtown St. Paul during the city's annual St. Patrick's Day Parade. The first such celebration occurred in 1851 and included the raising of the Stars and Stripes, speeches, a supper, and an impromptu parade of some three hundred citizens. At some point, Archbishop John Ireland decided his flock was having too much fun and he requested a halt to the parades, which he called "midnight orgies." The St. Patrick's Day Parade did not reappear in St. Paul until 1967, long after the Archbishop could protest.

Opposite: A twenty-two-acre wooded lot south of Shakopee becomes a European village of the 1600s during the Minnesota Renaissance Festival. Performers in garb of the era pop up everywhere, like this young woman at the Ballina Irish Cottage. There's armored jousting, seven performance stages, human chess games, a complete children's area, lots of food and drink, and shops displaying the wares of more than 240 artisans.

"Thirty-six years in this marvelous community have passed in a moment. They have been enriched by a marvelous arts community, excellent schools at every level, diverse population, progressive government, and exhilarating weather. Given any choice—we would not choose to leave." **Charles S. Anderson, Ph.D., President, Augsburg College**

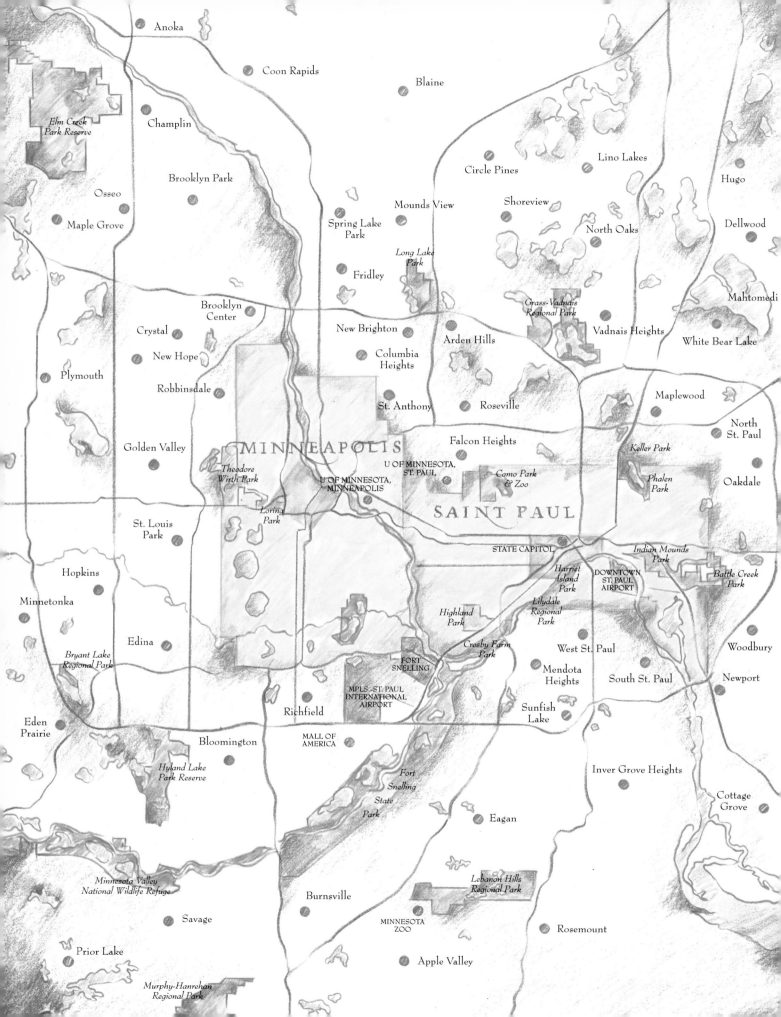

Anoka

Coon Rapids

Blaine

Elm Creek Park Reserve

Champlin

Circle Pines

Lino Lakes

Hugo

Brooklyn Park

Shoreview

North Oaks

Dellwood

Osseo

Mounds View

Maple Grove

Spring Lake Park

Fridley

Long Lake Park

Grass-Vadnais Regional Park

Mahtomedi

Vadnais Heights

White Bear Lake

Brooklyn Center

New Brighton

Crystal

Columbia Heights

Arden Hills

New Hope

Roseville

Maplewood

Plymouth

Robbinsdale

St. Anthony

North St. Paul

Golden Valley

Falcon Heights

Keller Park

MINNEAPOLIS

U OF MINNESOTA, ST. PAUL

Como Park & Zoo

Phalen Park

Oakdale

Theodore Wirth Park

U OF MINNESOTA, MINNEAPOLIS

SAINT PAUL

St. Louis Park

Loring Park

STATE CAPITOL

Indian Mounds Park

Hopkins

Harriet Island Park

DOWNTOWN ST. PAUL AIRPORT

Battle Creek Park

Minnetonka

Lilydale Regional Park

Highland Park

Woodbury

Bryant Lake Regional Park

Edina

Crosby Farm Park

West St. Paul

Newport

FORT SNELLING

Eden Prairie

Richfield

Mendota Heights

South St. Paul

MPLS.-ST. PAUL INTERNATIONAL AIRPORT

Sunfish Lake

Bloomington

MALL OF AMERICA

Hyland Lake Park Reserve

Inver Grove Heights

Fort Snelling State Park

Cottage Grove

Eagan

Minnesota Valley National Wildlife Refuge

Burnsville

Lebanon Hills Regional Park

Savage

MINNESOTA ZOO

Rosemount

Prior Lake

Apple Valley

Murphy-Hanrehan Regional Park